CAR

MUSIC

MUSIC

Jaq Greenspon

VGM Career Horizons
a division of *NTC Publishing Group*
Lincolnwood, Illinois USA

Special thanks to Willie Etra, who was invaluable in making this book come together. Thanks also to Joe Kuhr and Matt Green for being behind the scenes, and to Tony Breit for introducing me to music. And to Nic, just because.

I'd also like to thank Amy Yu, the designer, for making my words look so great.

Photo Credits:

Pages 1 and 15: Photo Network; page 29: American Conservatory of Music/Mike Tappin; pages 43 and 71: Photo Network.

All other photographs courtesy of the author.

Library of Congress Cataloging-in-Publication Data

Greenspon, Jaq.
   Career portraits, music/Jaq Greenspon.
      p.   cm.
   ISBN 0-8442-4360-4
   1. Music trade—Vocational guidance.   I. Title.
ML3790.G75 1995
780'.23'73—dc20

94-13634
CIP
MN

Published by VGM Career Horizons, a division of NTC Publishing Group
4255 West Touhy Avenue
Lincolnwood (Chicago), Illinois 60646-1975, U.S.A.
© 1995 by NTC Publishing Group. All rights reserved.
No part of this book may be reproduced, stored in a retrieval system,
or transmitted in any form or by any means,
electronic, mechanical, photocopying, recording or otherwise,
without the prior permission of NTC Publishing Group.
Manufactured in the United States of America.

4 5 6 7 8 9 0 ML 9 8 7 6 5 4 3 2 1

Contents

Awopbopaloobop Alopbamboom

—Little Richard

Introduction

Music is the universal language. Every day the radio waves of this country are filled not only with music that originated here, but also music from all over the globe. It is not uncommon for musicians from Africa and England to work with musicians from North and South America. Everywhere, people are making music. Some of them are making a living with music, and only a small portion of them are musicians. It takes a group effort to make a record happen and get it to the point where you can listen to it. The performers may be the best known, but they wouldn't be famous if a record executive hadn't found and promoted them. You would never have heard them if a disc jockey hadn't played their record. The record wouldn't have sounded so good if there hadn't been a great engineer and producer behind the sound board. So you see, even if you aren't a musician, the music industry is still wide open to you.

INSTRUMENT

MAKERS

D o you like working with your hands? When you hold a piece of wood, can you feel what it could become? Can you see the fine detail of a solid neck sliding cleanly into a body inlaid with a custom wood design? Can you hear the beautiful sounds coming from this custom guitar? It's all in tune, but it's not finished. It is only finished when you, as the creator of this fine work of musical art, put your finishing touches and your signature on it. That is how people know it's a one-of-a-kind creation.

1

What it's like to be an instrument maker

Most independent instrument makers start out as musicians themselves. Then they may decide their talents are better suited to working on the instrument rather than playing it full time. When they do go into business, however, the instrument making and custom work are only a small part of what they do. They will spend a lot of their time fixing equipment. This equipment could be from their own factory, coming back for repairs and adjustments, or it could be from somewhere else.

The pleasures and pressures of the job

Making an instrument is not as easy as it sounds. Most instrument makers would be very happy to just make their instrument of choice, but this is not very often possible. On the downside, they have to deal with customers and deadlines. As in any business where you are making a product for a specific person, there are some people you will never be able to please. They will always insist something is not right or that it be done over. Even when it is a simple job, the customer may want it done immediately. Sometimes this is just impossible, but you have to do your best to meet the deadline.

The rewards and perks

On the other hand, when a job is done well and on time, it feels great. There is a certain pride in having an instrument you designed being played by someone in a first chair in an orchestra or in a top rock band. Odds are you are not going to get rich as an instrument maker, but you can make a decent living for yourself, especially if your name comes to mean quality and craftsmanship within the musical community. If a rock star plays one of your instruments, then all of his or her fans will want one as well. Eventually, your instruments can become collector's items, highly prized and valued the world over.

What happens on the job

The typical day for an instrument maker follows normal working day hours. She or he goes to the shop in the morning and sees what work there is to do. Usually there are some repair orders stacked up as well as orders for new and custom instruments. These are all put in order of priority: The ones needed the soonest are done first. Once the assignments are handed out, the business of running the shop is dealt with and then comes any other work. The shop generally closes around dinnertime, when everyone goes home.

Making custom instruments

Custom instruments are usually made in an assembly-line fashion. Rather than make one every time an order comes in, the instrument maker will make several at once. Depending on the type of instrument, the maker may produce them before an order comes in, in which case they will all be generally the same. Or the maker can wait until a bunch of orders come in and produce instruments that are the same in shape but have specified custom work done, making each one different. The entire process of making an instrument from scratch can take anywhere from a few weeks to a few months or more.

Getting started

To make an instrument, you have to know how it works. You have to know the basic principles involved in tuning and repair before you can build one from scratch. There are a couple of different ways to learn this. One is to get yourself an instrument and take it apart and put it back together. Do this several hundred times, then work on doing fine adjustments and slightly changing little things. Do this until you know the instrument inside and out. The other way is to go to school for instrument repair, where they'll teach you a lot of what you'd learn the other way. You're still going to have to put together a lot of instruments, but this way you get certified experience.

Preparing to be an instrument maker

Since most instruments involve more than one material (except the brass section) and all of them involve assembly of little parts, there are a lot of skills you can learn to help yourself along.

1. Woodworking. Whether you're building a clarinet or a guitar, you're going to need to know how to use woodworking equipment such as lathes and saws.

2. Metal working. For the woodwinds, all of the key components have to be assembled and possibly customized. Guitars have all that fret work. Brass . . . self explanatory.

3. Electronics. Any electric instrument has some component you may want to eventually improve.

4. Jewelry making. The intricate detail involved with making jewelry translates directly to some of the precision work you are going to have to do.

Let's Meet...

John Carruthers
Instrument Maker

John has been making instruments, specifically stringed instruments like guitars and basses, for about 30 years. He really likes the challenges.

How did you get into instrument making?

I was a musician and lived in northern Canada; there weren't a lot of people who worked on instruments and I was always very mechanically inclined. Consequently, I started working on my own and pretty soon I started working on other people's. It got to be that I was doing more of that than I was of playing. I got a reputation going and before I knew it, I was pretty much doing it full time. I've been doing it for almost 30 years.

Is there any special training involved?

There are a lot of things you can learn that would be very valuable. This isn't just one trade; it's a mixture of a lot of different ones. You have woodworking, metalworking, plastics, electronics, and finishing. That's what makes it so challenging and why I like doing it so much. It's

hard to get bored because you have so many different things that you do.

What don't you like about the job?

It's very demanding. It takes a lot of concentration on a constant basis. I think the worst part sometimes is having to deal with the general public. They have unrealistic expectations of what people can do. It makes it very difficult to always please everybody. You try to do the best you can But every once in a while you get some people you can't please, no matter what. I'd say that's the part I don't like the most.

What are some of the benefits?

I'd say the most rewarding thing is that when you craft something, it's like a piece of art. You can take pride in your workmanship. You can look at it and see the fine detail, how well you made it, how nicely it's finished, how it sounds. Then you get the reward of listening to someone playing it. If the people who buy the instruments are happy with them then it makes you happy.

What do you see yourself doing in 5 years?

We're trying to get more and more into manufacturing instruments and less and less into servicing them. That way we tend to cut down on our exposure in dealing with retail customers. We see 4,000 or 5,000 people a year and that takes a lot of time. We found that it's more economical and more peaceful for us to just make instruments.

What kind of advice would you give to someone starting out?

Really learn your trades very well, because that's what makes everything else happen. Always have very high standards. Don't accept anything but the best that you can do. Always try to make it better than what you did before.

What's the most unusual thing you've ever done to a guitar?

We've made a lot of strange things. I had one guy who wanted a guitar shaped like a fish. His last name was Fishman and he decided he wanted a guitar that was shaped like a fish, so we made him one. We've made a lot of custom instruments for people, double necked guitars, things like that.

What's Popular Besides Guitars?

We work on a lot of other instruments besides guitars. We work on mandolins and acoustic and electric guitars; we build electronic stand-up basses. In fact, right now, probably a very large portion of our business is electronic stand-up basses. They're becoming very popular and a lot of major groups like Duran Duran, Oingo Boingo, Gloria Estefan, Bon Jovi, and Pearl Jam are using them. Right now we owe about 20 instruments that we haven't made yet. To make a stand-up bass we start off with rough lumber and cut it to size. We have some machinery that actually mills out little cavities inside. Then we glue a front onto the body and resurface it all so that it's smooth. We have a neck that we make along the same lines, where we take the rough lumber and we laminate it together. There are several machining processes where we shape and cut it out. Then it has to be all fine-sanded and prepared for finishing. It gets sprayed with a sealer before it gets its final color and finish, which has to be sanded and buffed. We install the hardware and the electronics, then we set it up and adjust it. Finally we send it off to the customer.

Let's Meet...

Mark Chudnow
Oboe Maker

Mark is an independent oboe maker, one of only three in the country. He has been making his own for the past 6 years.

What first attracted you to making oboes?

I started out as a musician in junior high and high school and wanted to stay involved in music. I thought it might be interesting to learn how to repair instruments. A few schools in the country do have band instrument repair programs and I attended one in Sioux City, Iowa. Once you finish school, there's still an apprenticeship that you have to go through to really get the fine points of repair. That's when I got involved with the oboe.

What do you like least about your job?

I'm always amazed by the lack of knowledge of the players about their instruments. They are spending all their time learning how to make music, how to produce music on the instrument, and very little time actually understanding how the instrument works.

What makes your job interesting?

What's most interesting for me, I think, is doing custom key work—sitting down and figuring out how to redesign something. It's all very self-taught. I've been doing this for 13 years. Six years ago I made my first oboe. I needed the challenge to move on. There are a lot of different things I want to pursue about the instrument, changes to make. Some of them are cosmetic, offering a little better design.

What does it take to be an oboe repair person?

A certain "persnickety-ness," attention to detail that one needs to have with this, along with patience—patience more than anything. I can't believe that anybody couldn't do this, as long as he or she was shown the right way and was patient enough to do it.

What advice would you give to a young instrument maker?

If you have a love for a particular instrument, stick with that. If you're spending 40 or 60 hours a week doing something, it makes life a lot nicer if you really enjoy what you're doing. Getting the basic working knowledge of the instrument is probably the fundamental thing in instrument repair because that's what you're going to need to know, whether you're building one from scratch or just fixing it. Go to one of the schools, then specialize in what you love.

How to Make an Oboe

You start with a block of wood, basically a foot long and 2 inches by 2 inches. The instrument is made of three pieces, a top joint, bottom joint, and bell. You're going to have two long pieces and then one that's big enough to turn the bell. The wood all comes from Africa and should be aged at least 6 or 7 years before you start working with it. If it's too green and too wet it starts cracking. You take the wood and put a pilot hole in it and you turn the outside. Eventually, I'll go in with a tapered cutter and put the taper on it. Once the outside work is done, I put in the metal fittings. Then all the tone holes have to be drilled. All the holes have to be in exactly the right place and all in line with each other so that all the fittings and keys will fit correctly. I buy my key castings from Europe. They send me rough castings and I have to file and polish and solder everything together. Start to finish, the entire thing takes about 3 weeks. It's a very gratifying thing to do.

Success Stories

Antonio Stradivari is one of the most famous violin makers in history. He was born near Cremona, Italy, in 1644 and fell in love with the music of the violin at a young age. When it turned out his fingers were not agile enough to play, Antonio began to study the instrument's construction and apprenticed himself to Niccolò Amati, himself a master violin maker. In 1680, Stradivari opened his own shop and started to sign his own instruments with a Latin translation of his name: Stradivarius.

Born in August 1909, Leo Fender perfected the electric guitar. Even though he wasn't a guitarist himself, the Fender-designed Broadcaster became the first mass-produced solid-body electric guitar in 1948. The Fender Precision, 3 years later, was the first electric bass. The new design of the Stratocaster guitar followed in 1954 and became the favorite of Buddy Holly and Jimi Hendrix. After the second world war, Fender experimented with electric pianos, designed primarily for religious services. In 1965, his company was sold to CBS and continues today to produce a full line of instruments and equipment.

Find Out More

You and instrument making

Top skills for instrument makers and where to learn them:

- Woodworking—Wood shop in school.
- Metalworking—Technical or trade schools; local colleges.
- Math—School.
- Practical physics/engineering/ acoustics—College.
- Electronics—Technical or trade schools.
- Computers—Technical or trade schools.
- Art—Art college.
- Design—Design school.

You can learn all of these skills separately as they apply to instrument making by apprenticing yourself to a master instrument maker. Check your local instrument repair shops for advice on where to find local masters.

MUSICIANS

C an you hum a tune? Do you tap your feet in time to the songs on the radio? Is your favorite class music? If you answered yes to any of these questions, you may be looking at a career as a musician. Musicians do a variety of things. They can play in concert. They can be studio musicians and just play for records. Musicians can also compose music for themselves or others to play. Anytime you hear a song, a musician had to play the notes.

What kind of musicians are there?

There are many different types of musicians. Each type has its own good and bad sides. Rock and roll musicians get to wear whatever kind of clothes they want when they perform and since they work late at night, they get to sleep late. But there is a lot of competition and it requires a lot of luck to become a rock star. Members of an orchestra have a slightly easier time getting work, since there are lots of places where orchestras perform, but they rarely get to play their own work and they have to wear formal clothes. Casual band members play at social functions where they have to learn specific songs for the occasions and must also dress up, but "casuals" pay very well.

Why it's good to be a musician

(1) Money. While it's difficult to make a career as a musician, if you make it big, you make it really big. Bands starting out work for as little as a few dollars per musician a night. The big-time bands can make millions of dollars. The average working musicians, though, make enough to support themselves without taking other, nonmusic jobs.

(2) Travel. Sure, the big bands travel the world while promoting their latest album, but what if you're not in a popular band? You

can still travel. Cruise ships, hotels, ski resorts, all of these types of places use musicians for everything from lounge acts to full production shows.

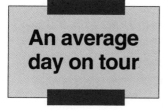

An average day on tour

Let's assume we're talking about you, a mega rock star who has just pulled into town. Your day would go something like this:

(1) Wake up late. Odds are, you had a gig (slang for show) last night and you didn't get to town until early this morning.

(2) Do a local radio or TV show. Meet with the press to promote your concert that night. Maybe play something live. Talk to your fans during question-and-answer time.

(3) Meet the fans. Go to a local record store to sign copies of your latest album and pose for pictures.

(4) Sound check. Check out the arena where you will be performing and where your road crew has set up all your equipment. Play your instrument so your soundperson can check his other equipment to make sure you sound great.

(5) Concert. Thousands of adoring fans are waiting to see you play the music you love so much. Give 'em all you got.

Getting started

Playing an instrument is something only a few people can do naturally. The rest have to take lessons. Schools generally offer band classes where you can learn to play, but that's not enough. You have to spend time after school practicing as well. Even members of famous bands and orchestras still practice several hours a week. If school isn't doing it for you, there are private instructors around.

Getting in the door

The best way to make it as a musician is to play as much as you can with whoever will let you. Play in the school band. Play in the marching band. Put your own band together. A lot of famous bands started out as a group of friends in high school playing at parties. If you can't find any friends to hook up with, check your local paper. If there aren't any ads looking for musicians, place one. Local theater is another place to hone your musical skills. Either offer to play in the band when they do a musical or volunteer to provide intermission entertainment when they're not.

How you know you're doing a good job

In a rock and roll band, it's easy to chart your success: The more people who show up at your shows or buy your records, the better you're doing. But what if you want to play in an orchestra? When you start out with an orchestra, you audition for the conductor. She or he leads the orchestra and is in charge of hiring musicians. If you play an instrument in a popular orchestral family, like woodwinds or strings, you are given a chair assignment. As you get better, your chair assignment marks your progress and moves up until you sit in the first chair. This means you are as high as you can possibly get in this orchestra.

Do you have what it takes to be a musician?

As a friend once said, "Good musicianship takes a bit of talent and practice, practice, practice." When you pick up an instrument, what you are actually doing is making an investment in your future. The skills you learn will be with you for a lifetime and the more you put into practice, the more you'll get out.

Let's Meet...

Willie Etra
Musician

Willie has been playing music for 30 years and for most of that time has enjoyed it immensely. Now he's doing it professionally.

Tell me how you got started in music.

I studied piano from age 8 and played in junior high school dance bands starting at age 12. I was forced to study by my mom. When I first started I was very interested and excited. The recitals scared me and made me uncomfortable, but I really liked performing where people, especially girls, could see me.

Did you need any special skill or training to make a career as a musician?

Music is a whole new language. Musical notation is how you communicate with other musicians and composers. If you're a session musician or orchestral musician, you have to read music without ever having heard it, instantly. As a composer, you write pieces without actually playing the instruments. You have to know how to write for those instruments and their limitations.

Where do you work?

I work at The Groundling Theater in Hollywood. It's a sketch comedy revue show with improvised scenes as well. That means the actors make up the skits as they go along according to audience suggestions. When each show starts, I play an overture, a 3-minute composition to work up the audience. Then, as the show goes on, I underscore scenes. That means I accent a mood for the scene.

What other jobs do you do?

I did the score for a cartoon. I get to write music for commercials, TV shows, and theatrical and industrial films. I was the musical director for a television show produced by a member of the theater troupe. We perform live shows for corporations all over the country. These involve composing new songs and sound effects. I also get to play a musician on camera for TV, film, and commercials. Sometimes I just lip-sync and don't really have to play, but I need to know how to play so it looks real.

Do you prefer to work by yourself or with other musicians?

As a composer and sometimes in multitrack recording I work by myself. But as a musician, I find it most satisfying to work as part of an ensemble. The interplay between instruments can be one of the most rewarding and creative parts of playing. The way somebody else is playing influences what you play and vice versa. It can improve the piece and make the song and the whole experience more exciting.

What I Did Today

I started today with a coffee milk shake and at 9 A.M. a
messenger arrived with a videotape to be scored and sweet-
ened. Since I had already seen a rough cut of this industrial
film, I had a good idea of my themes and orchestrations.
After I aligned the action, dialogue, effects, and music, I
recorded the instruments on a MIDI sequencer. Then I
sampled (digitally recorded) sound effects, in this case
various office machines and noises, also to be laid in the
sequencer. I control the sequencer with the time-coded video
to check my cues against the images. After making some
minor changes, I committed the whole thing to tape in time
for the messenger to take back to San Francisco. In the later
afternoon, I wrote out the music for my substitute at my
theatrical gig. This way, he could read the musical pieces in
addition to hearing a tape of the show instead of depending
on his memory.

Let's Meet...

Steve Clark
Drummer

Steve started playing the drums when he was 8 years old. He loves the fact that he gets paid to make lots of noise.

What first attracted you to a career as a drummer?

I felt I was naturally rhythmic. I was always tapping my feet to music. My third grade teacher thought that I should be a drummer—she noticed that I was always tapping things. So I got interested in it. It took a couple of years before I could talk my parents into buying me some instruments. Once I got my first drum kit, I immediately began playing. There was no coordination problem, I just sat down and started playing. I'm completely self-taught. Never had a lesson.

Would you recommend that?

No, not necessarily. I think you need to get involved in as many musical things as you can—every school band or choir, every possible opportunity to play. Play in everything, from the school choir or musical to the basketball pep band or something like that. The most experience you can get is what I'd recommend.

Should you learn to read music?

Yes. Every bit of experience is valuable. Even
things you wouldn't expect to be a worthwhile
experience still give you valuable experience
that you may use on some other type of music
that's not even related. Years later it can come
into play.

What do you like most about being a drummer?

It gives me the opportunity to travel around a
lot for different gigs. I've gone to many places
that I never imagined that I would go. I've
played in Jamaica, Puerto Rico, Colombia,
British Columbia, and Alaska.

What do you like least about being a drummer?

The work is not always that steady. You're out
there free-lancing and sometimes there are
periods where you don't work for a while so
you have no money.

Where do you see yourself in 5 years?

Probably doing pretty much the same thing.
I like what I'm doing. I'm not going to get rich,
unless I get lucky and lock onto some really
great gig someplace, but I can make a living.
It's important to have a whole bunch of different people who will hire you for different types
of things. That's why it is important not to
play just one type of music. If you were a
metalhead, you could only play metal gigs and
you couldn't play in a country band. You
should be able to play everything.

Is there some advice you can give?

Practice hard. Each step is logical. You don't necessarily need a teacher to teach you what the next logical step is. If you just think about it, you can figure it out on your own. It's important to get involved with as many things as you can in school and with extracurricular things, too.

Playing Freelance— Everywhere!

I've worked on cruise ships.

I've played for comedy troupes and theaters.

I've done jazz festivals.

I've played in rock and roll clubs and top 40 bands.

You might get lucky and get a job where you go to Orlando to work at Disney World or something like that.

Success Stories

Born in Berkshire, England, in May 1953, Oldfield started at age 14 in a folk duo with his sister Sally. He released his first acoustic album, *Sallyangie,* at age 15. At 17, he joined up with Kevin Ayres in Whole World as a bassist/guitarist. He hooked up with a new label on the strength of his 50-minute demo, on which he played all the instruments. The resulting album, *Tubular Bells,* has sold more than 10 million copies world wide, has a sequel album, and was used as the theme music for the movie *The Exorcist.*

Born in 1926, trumpeter Miles Davis has been incredibly influential in both jazz and rock. In 1941, he played with a local St. Louis jazz band and in 1945 he was sent, by his father to the Julliard music school in New York. He left Julliard to play with people like Charlie Parker. He started out on the definitive be-bop collection with Charlie Parker and changed directions a couple of times in the 1950s and 1960s when he tried more complex, or difficult, works using improvisation. In the late 1960s and early 1970s, Davis pioneered the fusion of rock and jazz.

Find Out More

You and musicianship

Top skills needed:

- *Sight-reading music.* Go to school and practice. There are also courses available. This is an advantage in getting studio work.

- *Skill on your instrument.* Learn your scales and repertoire (the music you play). If you are the best, you will always be employed.

- *Composition—the ability to create original works.* Play your instrument and practice.

- *Friendliness.* Be a nice person and people will want to work with you.

- *Flexibility/resiliency.* Being a musician is not a nine-to-five job. You need to be able to do whatever you can to work at your craft.

SINGERS

F rom television commercials to "The Star-Spangled Banner" to your favorite song, somebody has that microphone and is singing his or her heart out. In a band, the singer is usually right out in front, talking with the audience and getting the crowd worked up. At a ballpark, the singer is in front of 50,000 people, belting out the national anthem to start the game. On TV, singers are selling everything from hot dogs to lumber. All over the music industry, singers are the spokespeople, giving voice to the words.

The rewards of the job

Imagine listening to the radio and hearing your voice come out of the speakers. Imagine being asked to sing with people you've been a fan of since before you were old enough to buy their records. Those are just two of the things that can happen to you. Sure, you can make lots of money, but it's not likely. If you put out a record you'll probably make some money, but you'll also get to tour, meet fans from all over the world, do radio and TV interviews, and have a product that you'll be proud of and will last a long time.

Climbing the career ladder

As a singer, your career can go from nowhere to superstardom literally overnight. You can put out an album, or even just one song, have it hit the charts, and jump right to the top ten, but it's unusual. What you can expect is a lot of hard work, playing in small clubs for very little money. Once you sign a record deal, odds are you'll still play in the smaller clubs, but your tour may take you farther from your immediate area. As you put out more records, your popularity should increase and so will your audience.

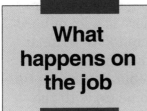

What happens on the job

As a singer, your main responsibility is to make sure you keep your voice in shape. While other musicians can play if they're not feeling well or even come back from serious injury, a singer must rely only on her or his voice. When you record, you need to warm up your voice so you don't hurt it. Singing in a studio is easier than singing live, where not only do you have to warm your voice, but your body has to be in shape, too. You need to learn breath control and how to sing without hurting your throat. It doesn't do you any good to be halfway through your show and be out of breath with a scratchy voice.

Training

Being a singer is like any other job. The hours may be a bit different and the fame may be a greater incentive, but you still have to learn the tricks of your trade. Talent doesn't mean anything unless you use it to its full potential. Every singer you listen to has probably worked with a vocal coach to learn breath control and technique. Vocal coaches are also helpful in honing your voice, bringing out all the finer qualities. They can teach you how to extend your vocal range and how to create a sound that is uniquely yours. You should always be willing to learn more about what you do.

The pleasures and pressures

Behind the touring and glamour of being a singer there is a lot of hard work. Most singers today write at least part of their own material. If they work with a band, then it's up to the group to come up with the songs for each album. This is done before the band and singer go into the studio to record. Once in the studio, a record can take months to produce and may involve hours of singing the same line over and over until it's right. The producer may want to try something different and you may have to change the song around to fit the new idea. But when it's done and you're back on the road, it's all worth it.

Life on the road

The best way to learn about something is to experience it firsthand. When you sing with a band, you have the most contact with the audiences you meet on the road. You can learn a lot about different cultures by seeing the ways different audiences react. You may find Japan a very exciting place, yet the audience is very quiet and reserved. The Midwest of America, on the other hand, may seem like another farm but the audience will be on their feet and hooping and hollering loud enough to bring down the roof. In either place, they loved you just the same.

Other aspects of singing

Nowadays, you can't be successful if you don't have a music video to accompany your latest single. As a singer, you tend to personify the music you sing; that is, people connect the singer with the song. Therefore, the singer gets featured in the video. Because of this, some singers have taken acting lessons and have even gone on to do some film and TV work. Also, a lot of singers write the lyrics for their songs, if not the music as well. They draw inspiration from observing things around them, books they read, films they see. It becomes very beneficial to have a well-rounded education so you can draw on many things to create your art.

Let's Meet...

Terri Nunn
Singer

Terri discovered her voice long before she discovered school. She is proud of the fact that her mom likes what Terri does for a living.

What attracted you to a career in singing?

Music was my friend. It was always there. We were a family that moved around a lot so I didn't have a lot to hold on to. I was always making new friends but music was a steady. My records were always with me and I could count on them being there. I listened to music: It was my baby-sitter, it was my friend, it was my teacher, it was my fun.

Did you go through any special training?

No. I learned from records. I went to a vocal coach after the first tour, because during it I was a total idiot and I blew my voice out. We were doing six shows in a row and I had no idea what I was doing. I didn't know what I was in for. That's where technique for singing comes in. I don't like technical singers; I don't like technical musicians. I think music is instinctual and that technique should follow instinct.

What do you like best about being a singer?

The communication of ideas, the feeling of singing, and the music that I'm singing to. I'm completely inspired by what I'm hearing. I love music. I'll play it and I'll just get lost in it; then I'll start writing. I just write what I'm thinking when I listen to the music. Then separately I'll play around with singing anything, melodies. When I find something I like, I'll just somehow put the words, or pieces of the words, to the melody and it becomes a song.

What don't you like about being a singer?

Right now I'm in a process like dating—looking for a band—and I don't like it. It will get me where I want to go, which is in a group of people that excites me as much as the first group, which was called Berlin. When it works it's magical, and since I left Berlin, I've been looking for that.

What about travel?

That's a lot of fun; I like to travel. It's not like I thought it was going to be, though—it's work. They're not paying me to enjoy their country. I have just enough time to get there and play and then I'm out of there. I get to see where I want to go have a vacation.

What advice would you give someone starting out?

Don't give up on your dreams. Doing what you love is the best thing you can do for yourself and for the world.

How a Band Gets Started

I just started. I was 18 when I decided I wanted to be in
a band. I decided that I would try. I might fail, but I
would hate myself for the rest of my life if I didn't go out
and try. I met John, a musician, and we formed a band
and started to play.

We decided to make a record. We made a single first,
which got college airplay, then we made some demos.
All our demos were rejected by every record company in
Los Angeles, so we put our album together ourselves.
We got an independent company to buy it and put it out.
Within 2 months it went crazy. They couldn't keep it in
the stores. Then all the record companies came back
and we got to pick the deal we wanted.

Let's Meet...

Russ Buchanan
Singer

Russ loves singing. Even if he wasn't doing it for a living, he'd be doing it for fun.

What first attracted you to a career in singing?

It was a natural outgrowth of playing guitar. I started studying guitar at 7 and was hooked. The singing part came when I was about 14 years old and in a band. The lead singer had to move or something and we had no singer, so I started singing. I was much better at singing than I was at playing guitar. Plus I enjoyed it a lot more.

Have you found that you needed any special training?

As far as doing pop/rock stuff, probably not, though I know that my training did help in that area, too. I learned projection and the mechanics, what goes on when you're trying to make a note sound good. I didn't study very long. I did take private lessons for about a year and they were extremely helpful.

What do you like most about singing?

What I like most is the variety. You never know what the next project is going to be. Sometimes, on the downside, it can be boring, terrible music; producers you would never invite over for dinner. Sometimes it can be wonderfully creative stuff that really needs you to make it work. Those are the best.

What is the most difficult part of your job?

Lean times. I've been lucky enough to always make some kind of living. Sometimes I get a lot of money, some years almost nothing, but I've been able to ride through it. The real downtimes are when the work just isn't coming. It's a very fickle business.

Are you glad you do what you do?

It is a rewarding choice. I talk to my friends who are unhappy with their day jobs. They're building anger and resentment with every minute and I've never had that in the entertainment business. It is always interesting. I'm so glad that I was able to make money doing this; it's an incredible thing. In a way I'm proud, because it's what I chose at an early age and it turned out to be right.

What's a Typical Gig Like?

There are many different jobs, or gigs. There are road gigs. There are "in town" gigs, meaning Los Angeles, New York, or Chicago. There can be studio stuff. On the road, you're kind of a traveling salesman. You have your itinerary: You know where you're going to go, you know where you're going to perform, you know what the show times are. Personally, I enjoy studio work more than the road. The road is just a tough grind. Ask any traveling salesman. The road turns the gig into a 24-hour-a-day job. On the bright side, though, is seeing new places and meeting new people.

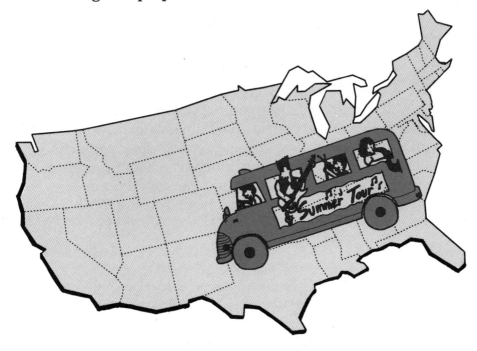

Success Stories

Defining soul music in the 1960s, Aretha was born in 1942 in Memphis, Tennessee. She mixed the unpredictable qualities of gospel with the sensuousness of rhythm and blues and the preciseness of pop. In 1967 she recorded 12 records, which sold more than a million copies apiece. At the time that was more than any other woman in history. In the 1980s, however, she sold even more by teaming up with pop stars like George Michael and Annie Lennox. Recently, Aretha has gone back to her roots and recorded an album of religious songs.

This Long Islander was born in 1949 and started playing piano 4 years later at the urging of his father. At age 24, Joel's first major album, *Piano Man,* was released, eventually earning him a platinum record. Never one to pigeonhole himself, Joel can sing in a variety of styles and writes songs that are easy to sing along with. His biggest hits are covered by many major artists and are quite popular among people learning piano. Joel continues to record hit albums and tour extensively all over the world.

Bette Midler

Born in Patterson, New Jersey, in 1945, Bette was raised in Hawaii. Named after movie actress Bette Davis, Midler took an early interest in acting. Her first venture into singing was an all-girl trio called the Pieridine Three. Midler played Tzeitel in Broadway's *Fiddler on Roof* before concentrating on singing. Her piano accompanist when she started out was Barry Manilow! Her first album, *The Divine Miss M,* went gold and won her the best new artist Grammy. Since then she has starred in a number of films, including the Oscar nominated *The Rose,* and released several albums, almost all of which have been best sellers.

Find Out More

You and singing

Why would you want to be a singer?

Do you think touring with a band would be fun? Why?

Where would you like to tour? Why?

Do you like performing in front of people? Do you get stage fright?

Would you like to be part of a band or sing by yourself? What are the advantages and disadvantages of each?

RECORD
EXECUTIVES

Music is a big business. Millions of dollars each year are spent by the record companies to promote and record their artists. Billions of dollars are spent by people like you to buy the records put out by the record companies. Someone has to be in charge. Those people are called executives and it is their job to make sure their company has the best bands around. The executives make all the decisions and if they like a band, they can make it No. 1.

Getting a head start

A record company is a business, and even though its product is creative, getting the product out is not. The day-to-day operations of the company are very similar to those of almost any business. To break into this corporate structure, the best thing to do is learn as much as you can about the industry, then offer your services as an intern. You won't make much money, but you'll be involved and meeting people. Most importantly, you'll have a record industry job on your resume. You'd be surprised to find out how much that helps when you're trying to get the next job.

Training

As with a lot of corporations, the more you know, the better you look as a prospective employee. Many of the people hired have law or master's in business administration degrees. A person with a degree will have the better chance, but you can also work your way up into an executive job, starting out in something as simple as a secretarial position. Either way, a knowledge of typing and computers is almost essential. The competition is fierce for these executive positions, so you should do anything you can to give yourself the advantage.

What it's like to be a record company executive

Generally, it's a lot like working with any other company, but you get to have gold records on the wall. There are a number of different positions; the one thing almost all have in common is that you do 90 percent of your work in an office during normal business hours. Occasionally you may go down to a studio to see how one of your bands is doing or even out on the town one night to catch one of your acts on the road, but most of the time you're behind a desk doing business.

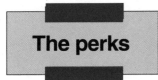

The perks

As an executive, you are in charge of anything from a department to the whole company, and you have people working for you. The money you make reflects that level of responsibility. Also, since you work for a company, you get planned vacation time. And because you work for a record company, you get all sorts of free music. The music industry is not very large and you will end up meeting people who work for other record companies. Through them you'll be able to get their companies' records and maybe even free concert tickets.

The pressures and pleasures

A record company's profits are based on public opinion. This means that if people don't like the record, they won't buy it. If they don't buy it, the company doesn't make money and you lose your job. Depending on what you do, you may have to decide how the record jacket looks, how the album should be promoted, or even if the band should put out another album. That's pressure. There's a lot riding on your shoulders. But if it works and the album's a hit, then you're a hit. You can take a great amount of pride when an album you had something to do with reaches No. 1.

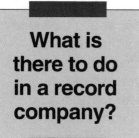

What is there to do in a record company?

There are several different departments in a record company, each with its own executives. Each also has a unique set of responsibilities within the company and all are equally important. Take a look at the different jobs and see which one fits you the best.

The art department designs covers and ads for the records and handles photographs of the band.

The publicity department puts out press releases to get the band noticed, sets up interviews with the band, and deals with journalists.

The artist and repertoire (A & R)
department deals with the band
and is responsible for finding new
talent.

The legal department is responsible
for making sure the band and
the record company stay legal. It
handles any lawsuits for the
company.

Let's Meet...

Wendy Weisberg
Publicist

Wendy is the manager of publicity for the West Coast for I.R.S. Records. She's been doing this for only a short time, but already she's making her mark.

What was your first job in the industry?

My first summer after college I got an internship at a small label called Metal Blade Records, which is really one of the forefront, independent labels for metal music. I did college radio promotion, which is not to be confused with radio promotion. College radio promotion is calling up college music directors and convincing them to play your records. You can do this a variety of ways. You can rely on your charm and wit, or you can rely on the music, which is the best way.

What did you study in college? Are you using it in your job?

I was a sociology major. Sociology is basically the study of groups and how they relate with each other, and I think I am using it. In my business, especially because I'm a publicist, I have to deal with a variety of people. I'm not just dealing with my boss; I'm also dealing with people around the office and managers of bands who can be very difficult sometimes. Excepting promotion people, I probably work more with the artist at this level than the people in marketing or business affairs.

What are some of your other responsibilities?

In addition to doing the phones, I'm in charge of keeping the books for myself and my boss in New York. I have to make sure the invoices are paid, I send things out to the vendors, I send photos out to be duplicated. I do bios, or biographies. A biography is a nicely written piece on the band members saying who they are and where they come from, and it's almost always one page.

What do you like most about your job?

I like talking to and meeting nice writers. It's always nice to find someone who is genuinely a music lover, someone who is interested. Someone who is fun, who wants to talk about more than just what I'm doing. You want someone you can relate to. Basically, the major tool of publicity is personality. If writers don't like who you are, then they're going to give you the brush-off every time.

What do you like least?

Writers who don't return phone calls. Writers who don't give me a straight answer. Some people will give me the song and dance. I want to hear some reaction, even if they hated it. I don't like beating around the bush; I'd rather get a straight answer.

A Typical Day for Wendy

I get in between 9 and 9:30 in the morning. I try to go
through my piles of mail. Then I go to my best little friend
here in the office, my tour itinerary, which lists the club
dates and towns all my bands are playing. Now I start
calling writers in those areas weeks in advance because we
need to let them know the band or artist is coming to town.
I make sure they have the album, the bio, and the photo and
try to set up a phone interview to advance the show, which
is the ideal situation. If it's a new record, I try to have the
writer review the record and tag on a bit at the end, saying
you can see so-and-so at such-and-such venue. At the very
least, I'll ask them to do a blurb or a photo. Sometimes a
picture is worth a thousand words. A lot of times, if someone
is looking through the local paper, just skimming, and sees a
photo of someone with just a caption telling where she or he
is playing, that will catch the eye more than a quarter-page
story.

Let's Meet...

Artie Kemper
A & R Executive

Artie fell into the music business about 9 years ago. He loves the late nights and loud music.

What led you to music?

I had a big crush on Joan Jett, actually. Not just Joan Jett, but Sheena Easton also—all the women in rock in the early 1980s—and I wanted to get in a position where I could meet the women I was wasting a lot of time thinking about.

What do you do?

Basically, I'm a liaison with the artist. My job is to keep the artist happy and aware that the record company is looking out for the artist. I flatter artists a lot, but they're great people and it's a lot of fun to be with them.

Are you responsible for finding bands?

Yes, I am. I spend a lot of time in clubs, listening to new music. I scout a lot of bands. You find a lot of bands in Los Angeles and New York; Seattle was the hot spot for a while. Pretty much anywhere

people are playing music. I do get to travel a
lot; I've been to clubs all over the country.

How do you know what to look for in a band?

Each band has to be taken on its own merits.
There are people who say there are trends and
you have to follow the trends. Those people are
the followers. They're looking for the next
group that's going to be just like the last
group. If I hear a group and I think it's terrific,
I don't care if it sounds like the last group, the
group from 20 years ago, or a group that we've
never heard before. It's all going to be on the
merits of the band itself.

What is your typical day like?

My typical day doesn't really start until noon,
because I'm up very late at night. I'm going
around to these clubs, I'm listening to bands,
I'm schmoozing and being schmoozed by the
artists. I'm usually up until 3 in the morning.
I'll get up about 10 or so, get the kinks out,
and about noon I start making calls. If there's
a band I like I'll call them, invite them to come
in, feel them out, find out if there's something
there worth pursuing.

What are some of the benefits?

It's being around these really great performers. You hang around with them and just sort
of hope some of the glitter rubs off on you.
How many people wouldn't give their eyeteeth
to say they were backstage with their favorite
band? Or better yet, to be the person who
discovered them.

What advice would you give?

This field doesn't have a direct career path. Go to work for a big record company, do whatever you have to do to get experience: be a gopher, run errands, offer to help in any way you can. Let the people you work with know what you'd like to do and eventually you'll get a break. Another way people get into music management is by being in bands or managing bands and getting to know the record companies. It is a business of who you know, of personal contacts. That may not sound very encouraging, but if you really want it, you've got to try. You just might make it.

Artie Listens to Music— at Work!

We get a lot of cassette tapes from bands all over the country who want us to sign them. These are demos and they usually have anywhere from one song to ten on them. They're supposed to give me an idea of what the band can do. My assistant and I listen to the tapes and choose the best ones. That's my job—picking my favorite music.

Success Stories

Born in 1943, David Geffen formed his first record company in 1970, primarily so he could put out a record for Jackson Browne. The company was called Asylum and when it was sold a year later it had the Eagles and Linda Ronstadt recording for it and was worth $7 million. Geffen's second record company, Geffen Records, founded in 1980, is now considered a major company within the industry. Geffen is responsible for signing superstar bands like Guns N' Roses and has spread himself into other areas. His film company made *Risky Business* and *Beetlejuice* and he coproduced *Cats*.

Born in Detroit in November 1929, Berry Gordy, Jr., had only minor experience with the music industry when he took $800 and founded what would become Motown Records in 1959. Before that, he had owned a failed record store and cowritten and recorded several songs for Brunswick Records. Motown fast became a huge success, responsible for recording such talent as The Jackson 5, Stevie Wonder, Diana Ross, Smokey Robinson, and many others.

Find Out More

Try being a record executive

If you love listening to music, but you don't want to make music yourself, maybe you could work as a music industry executive. Music may already be a big part of your life. Find out how big by answering these questions.

List five ways that you find out about new bands.

List five bands that you have "discovered" for yourself in the past year.

List as many people as you can think of who you have told about a new band.

Write a press release for your favorite band. Consider the following points while you are writing:

• What qualities do you think a band needs to be successful?

• What makes this band different from, and better than, other bands?

• How much do you know about the band members' backgrounds? If it's not very much, try finding out more about them.

ENGINEER /

PRODUCER

Your chair is comfortable. In front of you is a control console looking like something from the space shuttle. You are in charge of the studio starship. This is where all the sounds you hear on a record are recorded and it's up to you as a producer or engineer to decide how it is done. As the producer of a record, you direct the musicians to be the best they can possibly be. As an engineer, you monitor all the equipment and make sure everything is being recorded just as the producer wants.

Training

There are plenty of colleges that have courses in music production or even whole broadcasting departments where you can major in whatever aspect you like. At these colleges you'll earn a bachelor's degree and have to take other courses as well as the ones specifically related to your field. There are also specialized broadcasting schools that grant certificates and train you in nothing but music production or whatever your particular field is. Either place will help you, as will just doing it. Any experience you can get is a benefit when you try to get a job. With schools, your experience is concentrated specifically on what you want to do.

Climbing the ladder

When you set out to be an engineer, you are not going to just jump right into Michael Jackson's new album. There is a certain order most people follow, which gives them the opportunity to learn all aspects of the field and prepares them for the next step at the same time.

(1) Runner/office assistant. You'll run errands and answer phones for the studio. In your spare time, you sit in the control room during sessions and learn about the equipment.

(2) Setup. You'll help set up the microphones and equipment for the session.

(3) Second engineer. Here's where you will actually assist the engineer with the recording, asking questions and getting ready for when you can fly solo.

(4) First engineer. You'll start off with simple setups and not too many instruments, but you are on your own. Eventually, you'll move up to bigger productions.

The rewards and pay

Imagine having backstage passes to see your favorite band in concert and knowing that the album it is touring to support couldn't have happened without you. That's just one of the rewards you can get. If you are in demand as a producer or engineer and a particular band wants to work with you, odds are it is not going to come to you; the band members will fly you to them, and if the studio they like recording in is in France, then guess what? You had better get a passport, because you're going overseas for awhile. You can also make a decent living. Good engineers can make as much as $100 an hour while producers, in addition to a good salary, share in the profits of the record.

Is music engineering and producing right for you?

Do you like music?

Can you hear all the different instruments in a song?

Can you hear how all the different instruments go together?

Do you sometimes listen to a song and adjust your stereo's bass and treble to get the right sound?

Do you like tinkering with electronics and computers?

Do you get along well with people?

Are you detail oriented? Can you keep track of several things at once?

If you answered yes to most of these questions, you may have found your calling.

What it's like to be a record producer

You start the project by meeting with the band you're going to produce. You are there throughout the rehearsal period, helping to arrange the songs, commenting on the music and instrument choices, and possibly filling in some of the lyrics. Once the band is ready to go into the studio, it's up to you to find and schedule the studio the band wants. You also hire the engineers and any other musicians needed for particular sounds. During the actual recording, you oversee everything. Once everything is on tape, you and the engineer sit down and mix all of the sounds to the right levels so you get it just right. After it's all mixed, the company gets it and your job is done.

Getting a head start

Most medium-size or larger towns have recording studios, which are always looking for volunteers to do odd jobs. The more time you spend there, cleaning up or bulk erasing tape or whatever, the more time you have for asking questions and being shown how the equipment works. Often, you can spend time in the studio learning when it's not being rented out for something else. Another way to pick up some of the basic abilities is to work with the audiovisual department of your school. Setting up and running the mixing equipment for school assemblies and concerts can teach you a lot about sound mixing, as well as giving you experience.

Let's Meet...

Dana Sue Collins
Engineer

Dana Sue has been engineering songs since she could use her stereo. She says there is nothing like making a song sound right.

What first attracted you to a career as an engineer?

I used to listen to a lot of rock and roll albums, Beatles albums in particular, when I was younger. I liked the idea of having a part in music without having to play it. I thought it was neat that I could be involved with it, be part of the creation, without actually playing an instrument.

Can you go to school to learn to be an engineer?

There are different schools you can go to. The first classes I took were at a community college, which is a really good way to start. Sometimes you're not sure if you'll really like doing it and a community college is an inexpensive way to get into it. Once you've finished high school you can take a class for only a few dollars. It's a lot less expensive than going to a recording school, a school just for audio recording, where you learn how to do 24-track recording.

What would you recommend?

You can start at a studio as a runner. You'll just do errands for the studio and clean up; it's a training position where you learn how to do basic things first. They'll start you out making cassette copies, then you'll work your way up to maybe sitting in the same room with a session. You sit in the back while they're recording and you take notes on everything that goes on, so when they come back the next day, they'll know what they did the day before. Sometimes it's a different engineer or it's the same tape but a different client and you need to make very special notes. It's important to write your notes well enough that people can understand them even if they didn't go to the first session. Next you will work on very simple instruments that are easy to set microphones up in front of and get a good sound from. As you get better, you start working your way up to being a first engineer.

What's your work environment like?

Stressful. You have to really be sensitive to the way the clients are. Some clients are very uptight and the whole tension of the session depends on how the client is. If the producer is a stressed-out kind of person, not really confident, he or she tends to be hard to deal with. You've got to have a good personality—you have to be able to deal with all kinds of pressure.

How a Record Is Made

You start out recording just the instruments. Sometimes they all play at the same time; sometimes they'll record the basic rhythm of the song then go back in and overdub, or record more over it, like the lead guitar or any solos. The vocals are also overdubbed. The next process is called mixing. You take all the instruments that you've recorded and you equalize them—give them the right highs and lows. You put them through different equipment to change the sound a little bit. You mix all of this down to just two tracks, which is what you get at home. This is stereo: one track is right and one is left. That two-track master, usually on digital audio tape, is taken to a mastering laboratory, where they make the records or the compact discs from it. And you have a brand-new album.

Let's Meet...

Jay Lewis
Producer

Jay is a well-known and well-respected record producer who loves being creative. He's been nominated for a Grammy award.

What first attracted you to a career as a producer/engineer?

I started as a musician and somewhere along the way I wanted to learn how to be an engineer from a creative viewpoint. I went to work at a studio and ate and slept there for a number of months until I started to get somewhat good at it. Then I started taking projects and got successful along the way.

What does a producer do?

Producer is a very creative job; it's like directing a film. Sometimes you're doing business, but most of the time you're doing creative input. You're finding talent, working in the studio, working on songs, fine-tuning stuff, helping with the arrangements, getting things recorded, and judging vocal performances.

Do you have to be a good musician?

You don't have to be a super-proficient musician, but you have to know how to speak a musical language. The better you are, the better you're going to be as a producer. You have to be an avid listener. You'll have to study all the different music markets, or at least the ones you want to be involved with. You have to know how to communicate with musicians. If you're schooled in the electronics or engineering end, it's easier to accomplish your job.

How did you start out?

I was going on the road working with different artists, touring, then doing sessions as a guitar player. I went to a little studio where I knew some of the guys and just started hanging out there. When they needed extra help on projects I would do those and get the experience I needed. After a while you start to get a little better at it and the quality of the jobs goes up.

What do you like most about your job?

As a producer, I like being involved with the creative part of the process, with adding my two cents by changing a chord progression or helping with a lyric. You're quite in control of the overall picture you're painting and I like that. It's a nice position to be in. As a straight engineer, I have kind of a high-pressure job with a lot of long hours, working for someone else.

What don't you like about the job?

It's like anything that's self-employed. It's on and it's off and people should be prepared for that if they're going to get into it. And if they decide to take some sort of staff position as an engineer or producer, they should be prepared to do a lot of work that they don't want to be involved with.

What Is a Typical Day in the Studio Like?

Let's say you're doing one song for a movie. Prior to the studio date, you coordinate all the various performers, book the studio time, hire the engineer, and coordinate with the film company. Then you work on the arrangement. Once that is all together, you start your studio day. Basically, at the top of the day you have your rhythm section or the orchestra, whoever the instrumentalists are, record the backing track for this song. That takes, on a good day, maybe 3 hours. The singer shows up next and you work on the lead vocal performance for 3 or 4 hours. Once you get that, the singer can go home and background singers come in. Then you might have a soloist come in and lay down some solos. Now it's all on the tape and you sit down and mix it, meaning you take all of the ingredients and put them together in a fixed position that is the finished product.

rhythm section

Background singers

soloist

Success Stories

Born in 1926, George Martin was a record company executive who signed acts and produced their records. He was trained at the Guildhall School of Music. In 1962, he signed the Beatles to their first recording contract. Martin produced all the Beatles' songs from 1962, when they started, to 1969. He was responsible for the string arrangement on "Eleanor Rigby" and even played the harpsichord on "In My Life." It was his knowledge that helped the Beatles create songs like "A Day in the Life" and "Strawberry Fields Forever." George Martin also produced the hit group America.

Born in December 1946, record producer Phil Spector was worth more than $1 million by the time he was 21. He began his career as a musician and even had a No. 1 hit, "To Know Him Is to Love Him." When he moved into producing in the late 1950s, Phil worked for such greats as Elvis Presley and Connie Francis. In 1961 Philles Records, Spector's own label, formed; it had several No. 1 hits. In the late 1960s, after having semi-retired, Spector came back to produce records for the Beatles.

Find Out More

Engineering and Producing

You may never have noticed, but the names of the engineers and producer are usually given on an album. Look at some of your albums. Were any of them produced by the same person? You will probably find that if you have two albums by the same band they will have the same producer.

Producers and engineers don't usually get the same publicity as the musicians they work with. If you think the record was done well, you could write to the producer or engineer to tell them you enjoyed their work. They might also answer questions for you about how they made that album. Send your letter to the record company.

You can also find out more about record engineers and producers by writing to one of these associations:

Recording Industry Association of
　　America
1020 19th Street, N.W. Suite 200
Washington, DC 20036

Society of Professional Audio
　　Recording Services
4300 Tenth Avenue N.
Lake Worth, FL 33461

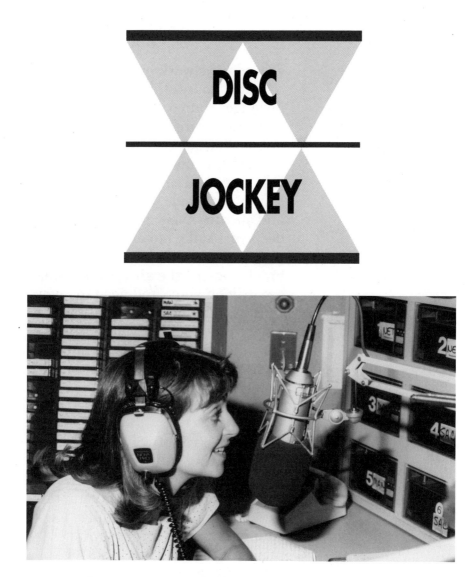

DISC

JOCKEY

I magine working in a place where you can say almost anything you want and people have to listen. You can tell funny stories, play the records you like most, meet and talk to your favorite celebrities, and even do weird and wacky things you've always wanted to try. To top it all off, you get paid to do it! If you love talking and listening to music, you couldn't find a better job. That is what being a disc jockey, or deejay, is all about.

When does a deejay work?

Disc jockeys work in shifts. Usually, a shift is no less than 4 hours and no longer than 6. Each shift, called a show, requires a slightly different approach from the deejay. If you work in the mornings, you usually talk more and cover more news. This is for people driving to work and starting their day. Lunchtime deejays usually have a special noon program for workers on their lunch break. During the afternoon, people are driving home and need to know traffic conditions and sometimes have a good laugh. Evenings are for people relaxing at home, and over-night shows are for an audience that can't sleep.

Getting a head start

There are a variety of jobs open to those starting out in radio. Before you get to put your voice on the air, you might be an intern or volunteer. Your job would include things like running errands or answering phones and taking requests for songs. You might get hired by a small radio station to be a board operator; you will sit behind the control board and do everything a disc jockey does except talk. You are responsible for making sure all the right songs are played and all the commercials are written down.

Pleasures and pressures of the job

The primary responsibilities of disc jockeys are entertaining their audience and playing music. On a day-to-day basis, this means following local and national news so you can update your listeners. You should also know as much as you can about the type of music your station plays. Your homework could include listening to a bunch of new records to decide if you want to play them on your show. You may even get the chance to meet and interview members of the bands whose records you play. However, most of your job is talking to yourself and hoping there is someone listening. There are times when it can get very boring, like 3 o'clock in the morning.

What it's like to be a disc jockey

On a normal day, deejays will start work by listening to their own radio station on their way to work. This way they can comment on anything that may have happened before they get on the air. Once at the station, they may want to check the various news services for the latest news or information. Most deejays have a box where their boss can leave them notes; they check it before they go on, just in case there's any change in policy. Once on the air, the deejay must make sure there is no "dead" air, or time when there is no sound. If no music or ads are playing, the deejay must be talking.

Getting started

If you know you want to be a disc jockey, start building your record collection now. You should learn as much as you can about all sorts of music. Even if you love rock and roll, you may end up working at a station that plays nothing but country music. You need to be prepared. A good training ground is college. College radio is a great place to get a lot of experience and to make your first air check tape. This tape is just as important as your resume; it is nothing but clips of you talking between songs. The program director will listen to this tape when deciding to hire you. The more experience you get, the better your tape and the more work you get.

Deejays do more than play records

Deejays don't just play records: they also do some recording. It is quite probable that as a disc jockey you will be asked to produce and record commercials, especially at smaller stations. This is where the experience from college comes into play. In college (or any broadcasting school) you are going to learn how to operate tape machines and soundboards. You will also have classes in how to write ad copy and the best way to record it so it sells the product . Examples of your best production work can help you get a job and should be included on your tape.

Is being a disk jockey right for you?

Would you rather listen to an instrument than play it?

Do you think your voice is pleasant and easy to listen to?

Do people like listening to what you have to say?

Do you enjoy spending hours talking to yourself?

If you answered no to any of these questions, a career as a disc jockey may not be the right choice for you. On the other hand, answering yes makes you a prime candidate for becoming an "on the air personality."

Let's Meet...

Johnny Stiff
Disc Jockey

Johnny Stiff has been spinning records for almost 6 years. He keeps doing it because people are still listening.

What first attracted you to a career as a deejay?

The idea that I could force my opinions in music upon groups of people. Seriously, I liked the idea that I could play what I wanted and that I could possibly influence what the people who listened to me listened to. If I could turn my fans on to what I thought was great, that would be cool.

Tell me how you got started in radio.

My friend Tom showed me how to cue up records, count BPMs, and mix records.

What does all that mean?

Cuing a record is setting it up so that it's ready to play. You have to drop the needle on the very beginning of the track, or song, you want, then back the record up, leaving the needle in the groove so when you hit the play button, the song starts

right off at speed. What you don't want is that weird sound you get when the sound starts and the record is still spinning too slowly. Mixing records is kind of an art. You have to know what kind of song should follow another. BPMs are beats per minute. They're used to figure out the proper music flow.

What else do you need to know?

Knowledge of music. I can't stress that enough. You have to be able to stay current with music trends. And you have to be able to play a set that flows well, one song to the next.

What is the worst thing about working in radio?

The worst thing is dealing with ignorant people who call in requests. Some of these people just seem to want to ruin my day. They'll call and ask me to play a song that my station would never play, like Whitney Houston on a heavy metal station, or they'll request the song that's on the air at that moment. It's like they're not even listening. That gets frustrating.

So what's good about the job?

The rest of the people that call. The bad ones aren't that many, they just bug me. The rest of the callers are great. I'll have people call to tell me I just cheered them up by playing their favorite song or that I'm the only reason they listen to my station. That's how I met my girlfriend. She called to request a song and we started talking. She called back the next few nights and finally I asked her out. We've been together since.

My Best Day at Work

The most remarkable thing that ever happened to me on
the job happened just recently. I was working a remote,
which meant that I was broadcasting live from a club, and
the crowd was going wild. I was up in the little booth they
had set up for me and the other deejay, and people were
coming up and requesting songs. Usually that's not a big
deal since we play what we want, generally. At a club you
kind of have to play dance music so the kids can dance—
that is why they're there, after all. Anyway, we had been
there about an hour and some girl came up and requested a
song by my band. She didn't know I was in the band or had
anything to do with the song, she had just heard it and
wanted to hear it again. It was great. I was absolutely blown
away by it.

Let's Meet...

Mark Thompson
and Brian Phelps
Deejays

Mark and Brian are nationally syndicated disc jockeys who have tried everything and done it live, on the air, for their fans.

What attracted you to a career in radio?

Mark: It's a fairly lucrative field to get involved in. There's no real retirement age to it, you can make anywhere from minimum wage to unlimited amounts of money, depending on what position you're in, you wear what you want to wear to work, and you get creative satisfaction.

Brian: What attracted me personally to radio to begin with was the idea of a job in comedy. What kept me in and why I developed a passion for it is that you get to create and you get to be different. That's why it's so attractive to both of us. We get to do brand-new things—some of them don't work and some of them do.

Did you have any special training?

Mark: The best thing you can have as far as broadcasting is concerned is a tape. If your tape sounds good, then that's all you really need; it doesn't matter what experience you have.

Brian: But school is how you get the tape now. They have great broadcasting schools and some big universities have great broadcasting departments. You get to go in the studio and sit in front of a microphone. What you should do when you get that time is not waste it. Don't try and be someone else; you just have to find what makes you different and cultivate it.

How did you get started in radio?

Brian: I came in through the back door. I was in a comedy group and we broke up. Then I sort of fell into radio. I got an internship at a radio station and realized that instead of writing bits for stage, like we were doing, you had to take 3 minutes and write something that has a beginning, middle, and end without an audience to react.

Mark: I did the "town to town, up and down the dial." This is the 12th city that I've worked in. You go from one station to the other and hope you make better money and get a better position.

What is the difference between working together and working by yourselves?

Brian: Mark had been in radio a long, long time and I had never been in radio. I had been in comedy a long, long time. We taught each other the first year or so, taking the best of what he knew and the best of what I knew and blending them together so you wouldn't know where anything started. Suddenly that was it—it was a "Mark and Brian" thing. Working together was a totally different ballgame.

What do you like best?

Mark: It's not monotonous. Neither one of us can imagine going to work in an office and sitting behind a desk and wearing a suit. That's our nightmare.

What Makes This Job Cool?

Brian: You meet people that you're honored to meet. You grew up with them as kids, on television or musically, and suddenly they're sitting in front of you and they're responding to questions and comments that you have, meaning that they're actually human beings.

Mark: Kenny Loggins came in and talked about his relationship and his divorce from his wife. The list is endless. Because of the program, we get to meet celebrities and bond with them.

Brian: When someone is a celebrity, a big star, automatically you think she or he doesn't have any time for you or isn't a real person, but I would say 95 percent of the people we've met have been surprisingly nice. It's just an honor to see that side of people, the humorous side.

Success Stories

Casey Casem

Starting as a disc jockey, Casem established the best-known top 40 radio program in the country. Syndicated nationwide, "America's Top 40 Countdown" quickly became a weekly staple of pop radio. Casem's demeanor, as well as his long-distance dedications, made the show a hit. The show moved to television for the successful "America's Top 10." Casem also made a mark for himself doing voice-over work on such famous cartoons as "Scooby-Doo" (he was Shaggy) and "Super Friends" (he played Robin, the Boy Wonder).

Allen Freed

Born in December 1922, Freed organized the Sultans of Swing jazz band before going into radio in 1942. In 1951, he created a show called "Moondog's Rock 'n' Roll Party." This was considered the first widespread use of the term rock 'n' roll. Even though Freed did not create the term, he is often given credit for it. What he did do was bring what was considered black music to a predominantly white audience.

Find Out More

You as a disc jockey

Have you ever heard the sound of your own voice? Did you like it?

What interests you in talking to other people?

If you could interview any band or performer, which one would it be? What questions would you ask?

What crazy stunt would you do for your listeners? What would you not do?

Could you share secrets about yourself with people you would probably never meet? What wouldn't you talk about?

INDEX